DENEKI

To Mark and Paul

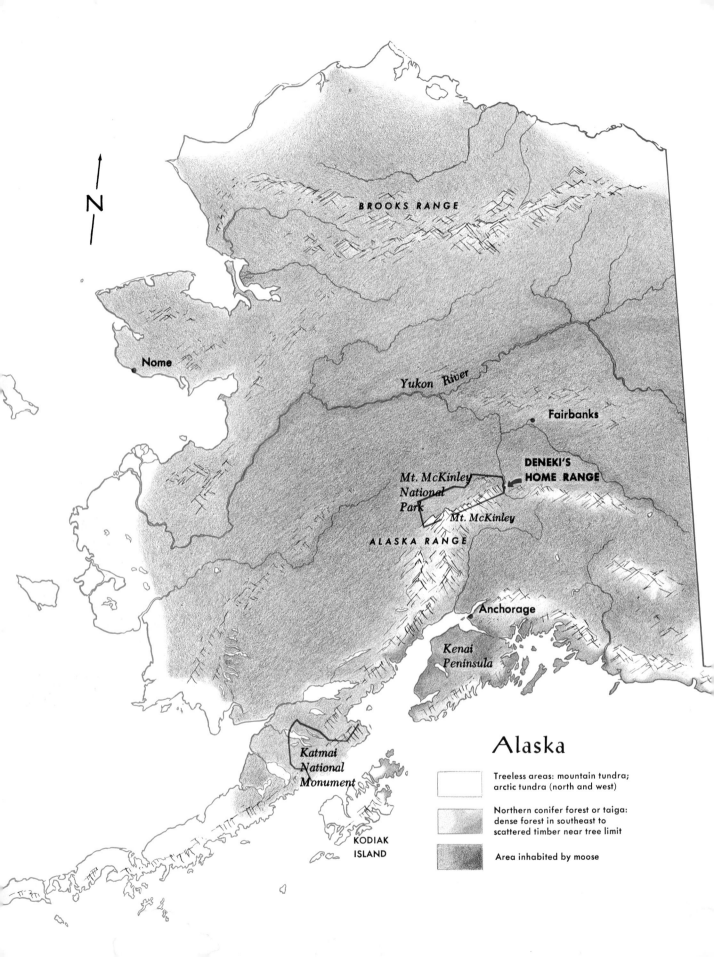

N

BROOKS RANGE

Nome

Yukon River

Fairbanks

Mt. McKinley
National
Park

**DENEKI'S
HOME RANGE**

Mt. McKinley

ALASKA RANGE

Anchorage

Kenai
Peninsula

Katmai
National
Monument

KODIAK
ISLAND

Alaska

Treeless areas: mountain tundra;
arctic tundra (north and west)

Northern conifer forest or taiga:
dense forest in southeast to
scattered timber near tree limit

Area inhabited by moose

DENEKI

An Alaskan Moose

Written and Illustrated by

WILLIAM D. BERRY

Published by
Press North America

Fourth paperback printing

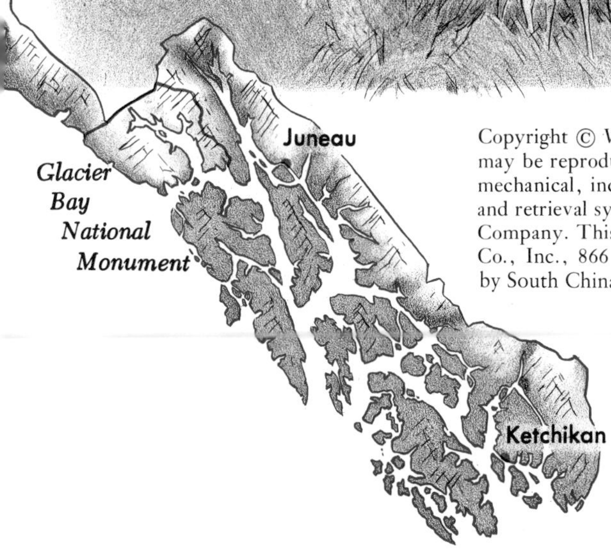

Glacier
Bay
National
Monument

Juneau

Ketchikan

ALASKA is one part of North America where vast tracts of land are still the home of large wild animals. Our story takes place in the mountains of the Alaska Range, in the valley where the Nenana River, flowing north through Windy Pass, marks the eastern boundary of Mount McKinley National Park. On the benchlands above the river just outside the park lies Deneki Lakes, a homestead beside two little lakes that are connected by a strip of grassy marsh. The name "Deneki" (dĕ-*nee*-kee), from an Alaskan Indian word for "moose," is well chosen; for of the many wild creatures to be seen at the lakes, the Alaska moose are the most impressive.

The "Deneki" of this story was one of these moose, a bull calf born and raised within a few miles of the homestead. He is named only for the book. Words and labels are human inventions, and no human mind can make more than an educated guess at how Deneki's nameless, wild world seemed to him.

Highway

The grizzly

Carlo Mountain, as seen from northwest shore of Deneki Lakes (circle below)

A ptarmigan's-eye view of the Lakes, from Carlo Mountain

Alaska Railroad

Nenana River →

Dry, open woods; shrubs, lichens

Bulls' battle

Dense woods

Marshy glades

The wolverine

Wet, open woods; mossy bogs (muskeg)

The wolves

Deneki was born in late May. Winter still clung to the cold north slopes of the mountains, but in the forest the snow had melted and swamps overflowed. Long days and brief pale nights were alive with the singing and squabbling of birds. Above all hung an elusive low, hooting, trilling note, the "wind-song" of the snipe, produced by the little shore bird's feathers as he circled far overhead. The sound seemed to have no source but to come from all directions—the spring voice of the northern forest, the taiga, itself.

At Deneki Lakes this forest is chiefly white spruce, climbing in patches and isolated trees to about 3,100 feet elevation before timber gives way to the low plants of the mountain tundra. Some of the tallest spruce, veterans of over two hundred winters, are about sixty feet in height, with trunks no more than two feet in diameter. Most of the trees are half that size or smaller—scattered spires that rise from a thick growth of low shrubs. Dwarf birches, usually two to six feet high, are the most common shrubs; beneath them blueberry bushes often grow. Below their branches—which are leafless in May—a bright evergreen carpet of mosses, cranberry, and Labrador tea, with patches of yellow-gray lichens, covers almost every foot of soil.

White spruce
Twig and cone, life size

Tracks in a moose trail: (A) Cow moose, trotting (B) Yearling moose (C) Cow moose, walking (D) Moose calf a few days old (E) Grizzly bear's hind foot (F) Winter droppings of moose (All shown to same scale; cow track 6 in. long; bear, 11 in.)

Few man-made trails enter these woods. The most conspicuous paths are made by moose, and these usually lead into willow swamps. Moose feed chiefly on willow twigs and leaves, and nowhere is moose sign more evident than among the dense thickets of one of these swamps. Heavy hoofs have cut a network of paths, 16 to 18 inches wide, deep into the muddy soil. All about lie piles of droppings, some old, some fresh. Broken branches where moose have browsed indicate the animals' enormous appetites and great size. Many shrubs have been topped at a height of four or five feet, and some taller branches have been broken six to eight feet above the ground in order to bring their twigs within reach.

Moose are the largest members of the deer family, but at first glance Deneki's mother—a cow moose six feet tall —looked more like a horse than a deer. She was feeding now on willow catkins. She seemed to move in slow-motion but for the rubbery tip of her muzzle, which flopped busily as she nosed among the twigs. She was more alert than she may have appeared, for around herself and her

RIGHT: *A 6½-ft. willow browsed by moose at (G) and gnawed by snowshoe hares at (H) in winter. Bird is a tree sparrow.* BELOW: *Moose antler, shed in December, gnawed by calcium-hungry rodents*

calf she was aware of an invisible circle, a territory whose outer boundary marked the extent of her interest, and whose center she would defend. Her mood was best indicated by her large, sensitive ears. When she was relaxed they tilted this way and that, taking in a medley of familiar forest noises. At any sudden change in this pattern of sound she raised her head immediately, ears forward in curiosity.

Now the switch of branches against some approaching form abruptly drew her attention. She glimpsed pale brown fur, but sight meant less to her than odor. Muzzle raised high, she tried to locate an identifying scent. She circled forward, her mane bristling as the intruder neared her zone of defense, and the splash of her hoofs as she crossed the marsh woke Deneki, bedded down nearby. He scrambled through the shrubbery toward his mother. The cow heard his bleating calls, and at the same moment caught the unmistakable smell of a bear.

This same grizzly had eaten a moose calf the spring before, while its mother circled and snorted, afraid to attack.
This time he was to meet a more aggressive moose. Deneki's
mother burst from the brush at the bear's flank, striking
savagely with sharp front hoofs. The grizzly swung to
meet her charge and rolled hastily out of the way. Once
she stood between him and his objective the cow moose
refused to retreat. She paced back and forth giving lowing
grunts of warning, her mane on end and ears laid back in
anger. Her threatening behavior convinced the bear that
he had lost the encounter. He bounded in a large circle
around the cow and calf, gave a few woofs of annoyance,
and lumbered away.

Deneki was only a few days old, but he was steady on
his spindly legs. As his mother set out for safer surround-
ings he followed at a loose-jointed bouncy trot, so close
behind he seemed in danger of colliding. She traveled

slowly through the shrubs with a steady, high-stepping gait, pausing occasionally while her offspring struggled through some obstinate tangle of branches. Just south of the lakes they came to a beaten trail and Deneki ventured a rickety gallop ahead. His exuberance ended abruptly at the marsh, where the path disappeared in a maze of willow, wobbly grass tussocks, and water. The cow moose plodded on, unaware that her usual trail was full of obstacles for a small calf; she waited while Deneki slipped and splashed to catch up. At the lake edge she stopped to assure herself no danger lurked ahead, then waded across. Deneki, suddenly out of the grass and up to his neck in cold water, discovered himself swimming. It was a skill inborn; he soon overtook his mother and was paddling vigorously close by. Near the spit of land off the opposite shore he passed her, touched ground, and climbed out to shake a spray of water from his coat. Just ahead lay their destination, the wooded peninsula between the lakes.

At the tip of the peninsula was a grove, almost surrounded by water and exposed to every scent-laden breeze —an ideal sanctuary for moose. Browse was plentiful. Deneki's mother fed or rested, chewing her cud; her calf, never far from her protective bulk and warm supply of milk, made countless explorations. He watched every movement, studied every sound, sniffed and nibbled at any object that did not move first. He was finding out about himself as well. In sudden silly frights and phantom battles —in play—he discovered the patterns of his own behavior, instinctive responses that were to be his means of survival. In his life there were no "rules" to memorize, for his rules were a part of his being. Under his mother's guardianship Deneki had time to find, by trial and error, how best to use them.

*Deneki's Battle with
the Gnarled Root*

Midnight on June 22, the longest day of the year

Green summer appeared in June, first on sunny foothill slopes, last on high ridges. Winter withdrew to its permanent lair in the peaks. The sun, dipping briefly behind the mountains to the north, scarcely seemed to rest now. Flowers came out, and on bright mornings insects flashed and buzzed among them.

A willow: twigs at right have been stripped by a browsing moose. Insects are a hover fly (below), mosquitoes, and a damsel fly (top right). Plant and insects are life size.

Cow and calf browsed in plenty. The cow stripped whole sprays of foliage with a swing of her head, but the shrubs showed little damage because she soon moved from one bush or thicket to the next. There was variety to her summer salad: willow, dwarf birch, some balsam poplar and aspen, and a garnish of fireweed, bluebells, and grass.

By mid-July pondweed grew thick in the lakes, and the cow came at intervals to feast. Ducking her head underwater, she spent fifteen or twenty seconds cropping a mouthful of trailing stalks, then raised up with a splash, munching and dribbling, before submerging once again.

Sometimes Deneki waded out and tried a few stray floating stalks, but he soon returned to shore. As a calf, he preferred less watery browse.

These aquatic pastures supported a diversity of life. Grebes and ducks that had nested in June now watched over downy fleets of hungry young. Some species sifted grassy shallows for insects, seeds, and vegetable matter, while others sought invertebrate prey in deeper water. Muskrats dived for pondweed shoots. Occasionally, gulls and terns circled over the lakes, pursuing mayflies, or swooping to dip insects from the surface.

Clasping-leaved pondweed

Arctic tern   *Barrow's goldeneye*

A moose's short summer coat makes bone structure and muscles conspicuous. A moose's nose, like a man's, is mostly cartilage inside, but a moose has a bulging valve (V) that can be shut to keep water out. Like cattle, sheep, and other deer, moose have no upper front teeth.

Muskrat   *Pintail*

Of the thirty or forty moose in the vicinity of the lakes that summer, all but the cows with calves led more or less solitary lives. Moose that gathered at the lakes came for pondweed, not company; they came at different times and usually left after an hour or two.

One July day about 2:30 A.M., Deneki's mother was the first visitor to arrive. She fed, ears flapping, amid a swarm of flies that glittered in the bright sunlight. Now and then she shook herself vigorously, for her short new coat offered little protection from bites. Next, two bull moose, a mature, six-year-old bull and a three-year-old, plodded in slow parade out of the marsh. They fed noisily, water cascading from broad antlers each time they raised their heads. Their soft-tipped antlers, now growing bone covered with skin and short hair, or "velvet," had been developing since the end of March, but would not be mature until September.

That day the afternoon temperature reached 78° F. Thunderclouds piled overhead, and the still air whined with insects. A yearling bull, wild-eyed, plunged into the lake, kicking and splashing; he trotted out drenched but more comfortable. At 4:30 P.M. cold wind and rain cleared the air. Deneki's mother reappeared that evening, and was joined by another cow, the mother of twins. The two cows fed in peace, although Deneki's mother laid back her ears once when the other seemed too close. By 11:00 P.M., in the cool blue dusk, eight moose had returned to feed.

At the end of July, Deneki's red coat was patchy with dark new hair; by mid-August he was sleek again in a new coat of gray-brown. One day a flock of baldpates appeared at the lakes and followed the moose for pond-weed scraps. These ducks had already flown from their breeding ponds; summer was almost over. Each night the darkness grew longer, and the long nights brought cold. Breaking clouds might reveal the first misty wraiths of winter rising over the water. Clear dawns had a breath of frost.

High-bush cranberry

Dwarf birch

Willow

Blueberry

During the last of August and the first week in September, the cool greens of summer were replaced by the brilliance of dying foliage. The domain of each plant species was marked in burning color before the descent of winter. First, rocky knolls blazed with ptarmiganberry; then dwarf birches and blueberry turned the landscape glowing red. Gold and greenish-yellow willows marked wet swales and watercourses. Damp alder thickets clung to their green until it finally dulled to brown. Spruce, unchanging, stood in stubborn dark contrast to this display.

Alder

Alpine bearberry, or ptarmiganberry

Now the rhythm of moose activity began changing to the restless tempo of the breeding season, or "rut." The bulls scraped their antlers against trees or brush to free the hard, mature bone of the dying velvet. Afterward, two bulls might interrupt their browsing to lower heads and clash antlers briefly, but these bouts were only mild preliminaries to the rutting ritual. About mid-September the same bulls, massive with fat from summer's feeding, no longer ate at all. Any bull that had not already found a cow plodded alone on his steady, single-minded search. Every few seconds he uttered a low, resonant grunt, and at regular intervals he stopped to look, listen, and test the autumn air.

One evening Deneki's mother, usually quiet, began to grunt and bawl loudly. Her wailing calls brought a yearling bull trotting to meet her. She laid back her ears and kept him at a distance, but he tagged after the cow and calf, grunting a response each time she called. He retreated next day upon the arrival of a mature bull, a 1,400-pound animal almost seven feet tall with antlers that spread five feet eight inches. The big bull approached at a swinging trot, and the cow allowed him a few introductory sniffs before cavorting away; she was not ready to be bred. He stayed close by, waiting, ready to challenge all competitors.

*A tree used by a bull moose to rub
velvet off his antlers*

The Defeated

A rival bull turned up in less than an hour, antlers gleaming as he paused to lower his head and thrash the brush. The contest began as a ponderous pushing match like most rutting conflicts, but — possibly because evenly matched bulls were disputing a claim scarcely established — it lengthened into violence. Bulky bodies pivoted and lunged; antlers crashed and clattered as each bull sought a weakness in the other's defense. The challenger, thrown off balance, stumbled, smashing timber as he fell. He scrambled up, dazed, then withdrew and went his way grunting, looking, listening.

September was hunting season. Men with rifles patrolled the roads and roamed the woods, each hunter hoping to bag his legal limit of one antlered moose. Late one afternoon Deneki and his mother were browsing near a seldom-used tractor road, the big bull close by, when they heard the labored grinding of an approaching truck. The cow trotted away, and the bull followed her. Deneki, hurrying to catch up, crossed the road just as the truck came into view. Two men were inside, and the driver slammed on the brakes when he saw the calf, for if its mother were nearby there might be a bull as well. Before he had time to look, the other hunter had leaped from the truck and taken quick aim at Deneki. The driver stopped his companion from shooting, but the other swore that he had seen antlers through his sights. By the time the sound of human voices had subsided, the moose were a safe distance away. The cow and calf relaxed and bedded down. The bull remained standing, alert for any approaching rival, but unaware of the full danger of his recent experience.

Forty minutes later the sound of rifle fire brought the

cow and calf hastily to their feet. The two hunters, return-
ing to the truck after a hike down the road, had spotted a
young bull about three hundred yards away. No further
disturbance followed the shooting, however, and the three
moose relaxed again. The hunters were busy for the next
five hours skinning the carcass, cutting it up, and hanging
six hundred pounds of meat to cool. The cow and Deneki
were browsing almost two miles away by the time the men
finally set up camp for the night.

Jays and magpies discovered the camp at daybreak, and
were flying back and forth, carrying away bits of meat
and caching them in the trees, when the hunters awoke.
One man started shooting at the birds for target practice,
but the other persuaded him to set up an empty fuel can
for a target instead. Long after the hunters had departed,
and the last remnants of their kill had been cleaned up by
scavengers, the can, rusting, remained to mark the site of
the encounter.

Winter drew closer with each passing snowstorm. Frost stilled insect wings and each day in late September dawned on fewer migrant birds; summer's departing chorus left the stage to piping chickadee and raven's croak. On clear mornings the lakes might be iced across. They melted back daily until the sharp, frosty morning of October 11th, when a quarter-inch-thick sheet of ice stilled all ripples and held against water, wind, and a diminishing sun. A solitary whistling swan, winging late for the south, mistook the clear ice for water and crash-landed; it soon flew on through Windy Pass.

Rutting season had waned in the first week of October. Many cow moose had been bred, the bulls had begun to feed again, and moose once again went separate ways. Deneki's mother made one late visit to the lakes. At the edge of the marsh the ice, weakened by heat reflected from the mud, broke beneath her tread. She smelled pondweed, and spraddled down for a final morsel before abandoning the aquatic pastures until next year.

In his sixth month Deneki stood about five feet tall, and had a thick coat of long, coarse hair, ready for winter's deepest cold. Cow and calf now cropped the bare, dormant twigs — willow, dwarf birch, and sometimes alder — that made up their diet almost nine months of the year. If thirsty, they scooped mouthfuls of snow. They led an easy life along the upper edge of the forest, browsing two or three days near one frost-twigged thicket before drifting on to the next. Short days might be enlivened by twittering flocks of redpolls searching for alder cones, and long hours of darkness might see clear heavens crossed by the towering pale banners of the northern lights.

Passing snowstorms quietly built their intricate white architecture on twigs and branches, but wind soon dislodged their work. Snowfall at the lakes, as over much of Alaska, is relatively light. At the end of November about seven inches of snow lay in the woods, piling deeper only where wind was making drifts. Most of the forest remained in cold shadow. The sun appeared but briefly over the mountains to the south, and the weak sunlight seemed to have lost all warmth. Air temperatures that dropped during cold clear nights to 10° or 20° F. below zero might fail to rise for many days.

A moose-browsed willow branch: (A) Freshly browsed twigs (B) Old browse (The remaining twigs were not eaten because they were dead and dry.) (C) A branch from a tall willow, dropped by a moose and then gnawed by a snowshoe hare (All shown life size.)

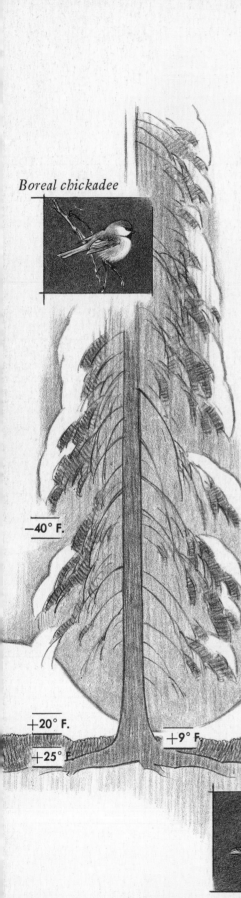

Boreal chickadee

−40° F.

+20° F.

+25° F.

+9° F.

The coldest days that winter came in mid-December. Skies cleared after a heavy snowfall, and the temperatures fell from near zero to hover near 40° F. below. Trees and bushes balanced their snowy burden day after day, undisturbed by any breeze. The very air seemed frozen. The moose browsed cold, brittle twigs or lay down, long legs folded against the warmth of their bodies, to chew their cuds or sleep under a cloudless sky. Their size helped keep them warm, for the greater an animal's bulk the more slowly it cools off. Under thick coats the moose lost scarcely any body heat. Tiny mammals, such as shrews and voles, would have frozen quickly had they not stayed beneath the insulating blanket of snow and moss, living in a little climate that could be warmer by as much as 65 degrees. Red squirrels were the smallest rodents to face the cold, but once temperatures had fallen to 25° or 30° F. below zero they also retreated under the snow. The smallest creatures abroad were chickadees, mouse-sized but warm enough because they could regulate the amount of heat produced by their tiny bodies and conserve it inside a fluffy ball of downy plumage.

After eight days, the cold snap broke. Warm air moved in from the south, roaring a gale through Windy Pass. Snow seemed to explode from the trees as the wind struck one part of the forest, then another. Air temperature rose past freezing and in a few hours stood at 34° F. above zero, an increase of 74 degrees.

Red squirrel

Northern red-backed vole

December 22nd, the shortest day of the year, dawned about 8:45 A.M., but the sun did not shine on the lakes until just past noon. A little flock of spruce grouse whirred from the peninsula to the west shore to feed in a sunlit tree. They walked chicken-like along the branches pecking off tips of spruce needles, their beaks making a steady, dry, snipping sound in the cold air. About 2:30 P.M. the sun completed its low arc and disappeared into bright sunset clouds. The grouse had gone to roost by the time the first stars came out, just before 4:00 P.M.

|← 4½ in. →|

A wolf track

March brought biting north winds and heavy snowstorms. Snow began to drift deep along the foot of the mountains. Early one morning, four wolves, following a moose trail because it made a good path through soft snow, came upon Deneki and his mother. The big wolf in the lead detoured past them; the cow's quick rise and threatening pose had told him they would make no easy prey. Two young wolves bounded closer, but soon hastened after their elders. Unless a moose showed signs of weakness or other handicap, cautious wolves preferred to hunt the less dangerous caribou.

Deep snow soon drove the moose down from the hills. Near one swamp where they fed, a wolverine loped hurriedly by so often that they soon paid little attention to him. He had found a moose carcass frozen under the snow, and now each day the warm spring sun was exposing more of his prize to hungry foxes, magpies, ravens, and jays. While he was busy chasing one away, the others feasted. By mid-April the twenty-five-pound wolverine and his unwanted guests had reduced four hundred pounds of moose to a few inedible scraps.

(A) Moose carcass (B) Wolverine's old, collapsing tunnels (C) Wolverine trails (D) Wolverine den (E) Fox trail (F) Wolverine's "scent post" or territory marker (G) Meat cached in snow by wolverine (H) A bone dropped by a departing raven

In April, days grew long again. Grizzlies woke from a six-month sleep; and golden eagles, circling high above bright sunlit ridges, drifted lazily northward.

For moose this was often the hardest time of the year. By spring, snow cover at the lakes usually averaged between two and three feet in depth, which hardly hindered these long-legged deer. This year over three feet lay in sheltered woods, and deep drifts in the open made any travel difficult. The snow began to thaw and settle on warm days, but at night or in cold weather, the damp crystals froze in a hard crust. Sometimes this surface was firm enough to support Deneki for a short distance; but it soon collapsed, and its broken, jagged edges scraped at every step. To cross deep drifts, cow and calf had to plunge laboriously. They traveled as little as possible, breaking down willows to strip every twig before hunger drove them to seek another thicket. The cow's bones began to show under her thick coat; now wolves, running lightly over the crust, might make a kill. It was the combination of snow conditions, available food, and predators, rather than any one of these, that determined the number of moose that could live in the valley.

Where one moose led, another followed; one moose trail often joined another. By early May the cow and her calf had made their way to the south-facing hillsides north of the lakes, where the snow disappeared first. Here little groups of moose had gathered on the warm, sunlit slopes. Their long winter was over.

As snow vanished from the woods, the moose returned to old haunts. Although Deneki sometimes browsed some distance from his mother, he still tagged at her heels when they traveled. In mid-May this pattern changed abruptly. The cow laid back her ears whenever he came close and struck with sharp hoofs if he persisted in following. She was about to give birth. Already her "zone of defense" centered around the unborn calf and excluded Deneki as an unwanted adult. His period of protection had come to an end.

Like many yearlings, Deneki appeared to feel more comfortable in the vicinity of another moose, for after a few days alone he formed a distant sort of companionship with an old bull. This big bull had survived battles and avoided hunters to reach a ripe maturity. Perhaps, if the young bull wandered the same paths, he might do as well; but this future was far beyond Deneki's understanding. He interrupted his browsing to scratch the tender knob of a new antler, then meandered slowly on to investigate the next willow shrub.

WILLIAM D. BERRY (1926–1979), well-known Alaskan artist and illustrator, left a legacy of outstanding wildlife art. This heritage includes the 11 x 28 foot mural, "An Alaskan Fairy Tale," in the Berry Room of the Fairbanks Noel Wein Public Library, *Mammals of the San Francisco Bay Region* (Univ. of California Press), and this book, *Deneki*, claimed by many to be the best of his books.

Bill Berry was born in California, studied at the Art Center of Los Angeles, at the School of Allied Arts in Glendale, at Glendale Junior College and at the University of Alaska, Fairbanks.

His career in art and illustration is widely varied, with museum curatorial work in Sacramento and as a preparator for the National Park Service. He was a technical consultant for Disney Enterprises in 1956 and 1957. He has taught at Tanana Valley Community College in Alaska. But much of his work was done as a freelance artist.

Bill's home was in Fairbanks. He and his wife Liz lived at Deneki Lake just outside Mt. McKinley National Park from 1961 to 1965 during which he researched and accomplished the book's art. Bill loved this country and this book can help those of all ages love and remember the great land of Alaska.

ACKNOWLEDGMENTS:

The author expresses his appreciation to Dr. Adolph Murie for criticism and advice during the preparation of the text; to Dr. William O. Pruitt, Jr. and Dr. Leslie A. Viereck for technical information and opinion; to Charles J. Ott, Warren Steenbergh, and Cecil Rhode for photographs useful in the execution of the illustrations; to Jon and Jill Gardey for help with each stage of this book, particularly the editing of the manuscript; and to my wife, Liz, for a devotion to all things Alaskan that led to the book's existence. Special thanks go to William J. Nancarrow, owner of Deneki Lakes, without whose hospitality, skills, and knowledge the work could never have been accomplished. Acknowledgment is due also to the many Alaskans who provided information, suggestions, or ideas that have influenced the shape of the story. Credit should be given to the amazingly cooperative assemblage of wild animals who served, unknowingly, as models.